Pim and Big Mag

By Sally Cowan

The sun is up.

Get up, Pim!
Let us go and get bugs.

Pim got up.

Pim and Bub sat.

Sim got a bug.

But Sim did not see
Big Mag on the tap.

Big Mag can see Bub.

Big Mag is fit!

He can get Bub!

But Pim can see Big Mag.

Pim nips him!

Sim got up to Pim.

Pim got a big bug.

And she got a bug for Bub!

CHECKING FOR MEANING

1. Where was Big Mag sitting? *(Literal)*

2. What did Pim do to stop Big Mag getting Bub? *(Literal)*

3. Why couldn't Pim and Sim both go to get bugs at the same time? *(Inferential)*

EXTENDING VOCABULARY

bug	Look at the word *bug*. What word would you make if you added an *s* to the end of *bug*? How would this change the meaning?
get and **got**	What are the sounds in *get* and *got*? Which sound is different? Use each word in a sentence to show how to use it correctly.
sun	Look at the word *sun*. It is a base for the word we use to describe when the *sun* is shining. What is this word?

MOVING BEYOND THE TEXT

1. What time of day do you think it is in the story? Why?

2. Talk about bird nests. Where are they built? What are they made of?

3. How do birds look after their babies?

4. What do birds like to eat?

SPEED SOUNDS

Dd	Jj	Oo	Gg	Uu		
Cc	Bb	Rr	Ee	Ff	Hh	Nn
Mm	Ss	Aa	Pp	Ii	Tt	

PRACTICE WORDS

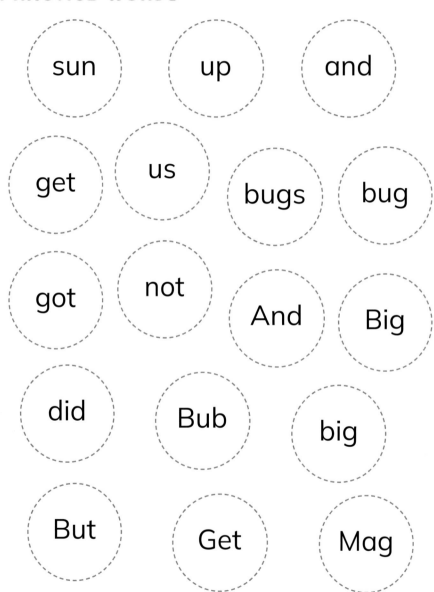

sun

up

and

get

us

bugs

bug

got

not

And

Big

did

Bub

big

But

Get

Mag